It's Got To Taste Good!
Easy Plant-Based Meat Recipes for the Adventurous Home Cook

Keep fighting the
good fight!
Libby and
Elaine

It's Got To Taste Good!
Easy Plant-based Meat Recipes for the Adventurous Home Cook
by Elaine Spencer, Libby Doughty and Annie Oliverio

Cover, Interior Design, & Photos: Ann S. Oliverio
Publisher: Elaine Spencer, Libby Doughty, Ann S. Oliverio
ISBN: 978-0-692-94076-1

1. cookbook 2. vegetarian & vegan 3. vegan

First Edition

This book is dedicated to all those who suffer and do not have a voice. We have not forgotten you. We will continue the fight until the factory farming and cruelties end.

"The greatness of a nation and its moral progress can be judged by the way its animals are treated." - *Mahatma Gandhi*

Introduction

In the 21st Century it no longer makes sense to pair the word "deprivation" with the words "vegan diet." Plant-based eating has truly come into its own with professional chefs and home cooks alike creating and preparing meals that rival anything meat-based. It's not just the general public, either, that is embracing a more plant-centric diet. Both old megalith food companies *and* new start-ups recognize the interest in, and demand for, cruelty-free, whole food products. It seems like every day there's something new on the supermarket shelf. What this means – beyond the joy of more variety for everyone – is that for those on the fence about making a switch to a plant-based diet, the excuses to keep eating animal products are evaporating.

Think you can't live without cheese? Stroll past the vegan "dairy" case at many major grocery chains and you might spy twelve different companies producing high-quality vegan cheeses including brie, cheddar, Parmesan, feta and mozzarella. Nearly everything you would find in a specialty dairy cheese shop!

What about eggs? Not a problem. That particular hankering can be satisfied in any number of tasty ways. The *aquafaba* (a.k.a. bean water) phenomenon that took the Internet by storm in 2015 gifted us with an ingenious way to create light and airy meringues and decadent chocolate mousse. For scrambled eggs, crumbled tofu is the classic choice, of course. Chickpea flour does a remarkable imitation of omelets, and commercial products are now available that eerily mimic the look, taste, and texture of that morning staple.

Going vegan doesn't mean going without your favorite warm weather treats, either. There are so many brands offering traditional and exotic flavors of ice cream now – a true embarrassment of riches! Even *Ben & Jerry's* has entered the market with several non-dairy flavors. It's all thanks to rich, creamy and versatile coconut, cashew, rice, almond, hemp, flax, and soy milks.

And finally, what about the main star and center attraction on the typical American plate: meat? Covered. With "chicken," "sausage," "pulled pork," "pepperoni," "bacon," and even juicy burgers that "bleed" just like their animal-based counterparts.

Within the past 5 years alone the number and variety of plant-based products has skyrocketed, landing into mainstream supermarkets and online stores like a breath of fresh air – at least for those of us who can recall less abundant days. All of this progress means two glorious things for the home cook: a plethora of ready-made vegan products to help get meals on the table faster, and ready availability of what were once novelty ingredients, to make plant-based cheese, eggs, ice cream, and meats in their own kitchens.

Of course, the beauty of that is that the cook controls the flavors, the quantity and most importantly, the ingredients. Commercial products, while undeniably convenient (and very often tasty), can contain ingredients that we have difficulty pronouncing and that we may be striving to avoid such as excess salt, sugars, added oils, preservatives, fillers and stabilizers.

Here's the thing. With just a little extra time in the kitchen, easy-to-find ingredients and basic equipment, you can make your own healthy meat "substitutes," and take pride in the fact that you are serving delicious food. That's what *It's Got To Taste Good!* is all about. We want to give the do-it-yourself home chef, the renegade kitchen adventurer, or the vegan-curious easy, flavorful and satisfying "meat alternative" recipes that taste great and are comfortingly familiar – such as barbecue brisket, hot dogs, bacon, burgers, and breakfast sausage. We also want to help you serve non-vegans such amazing food that they begin to question why they continue to eat animal products. Show them there is an abundance of cruelty-free options that meet and exceed nutritional, taste, and even emotional needs.

So what is it that makes a "meat" dish taste good? When you think about it, the flavor doesn't come from meat. In fact, meats from animals tend to be neutral in flavor as compared to plants. It's just as Chef Landau says. It's the spices, herbs, dressings and marinades with which one flavors food that create connections craved over one's lifetime. Tangy barbecue = tomato, vinegar, and brown sugar. Bacon = smoke, maple and black pepper. Sausage = fennel, salt, and red pepper flakes. These same flavors can easily be applied to plant-based recipes. There are endless possibilities! It's truly an exciting time to be vegan.

If you are just starting out on a plant-based diet or looking for ways to increase your intake of whole foods, don't focus on the things you are "missing." Recognize and appreciate the diverse and delicious world of edible plants and the unlimited number of ways they can be prepared, flavored, and served. We are just scratching the surface in *It's Got To Taste Good!*.

There's also a myth that plant-based eating is expensive and that preparing meals is time-consuming. We believe after spending some time with this book, you'll think otherwise. With the easy and approachable techniques shared here, it's our belief that you will feel confident enough to modify our recipes, or even better, to feel inspired to create your own cruelty-free meats (and cheeses, too!). *It's Got To Taste Good!* just might spark - or re-spark - your passion for food. Let us show you how to cook wholesome, satisfying and meaty meals at home instead of opting for less-than-healthy fast food or carry-out.

One last thing before we dive in to re-invent and re-imagine some meat-based favorites: the recipes here were not specifically created for this book, but rather are reliable staples in our own homes. Many of them have been crafted and tweaked over several years and have graced both weekday meals and holiday celebrations. We hope that you enjoy them with family and friends at your table.

- Elaine, Libby & Annie

Groceries

In our endeavor to simplify and streamline the recipes in this book, we focused not only on technique, but also on ingredients. "No weird ingredients" was our mantra. However, "weird" is a relative term. Before going plant-based, "nutritional yeast" sounds quite bizarre. Afterwards, many of us can't imagine cooking without it.

So our guideline was to only use ingredients that one can generally find in a typical neighborhood grocery store. Although some of these items might not have been available five years ago, plant-based cooking is gaining ground and local markets are starting to carry more items. Many of these foods have been hiding all along on the grocery shelves. You probably didn't see them because you didn't have a reason to look.

Now that you *are* looking, here is some information to help you find and use the ingredients that might have gone unnoticed before going vegan.

Almond Meal

Almond meal is what it sounds like – ground up almonds. Notice that meal is not the same as almond flour. Flour is ground to a powder and is made from blanched almonds. Meal is coarse and includes the almond skins. Almond meal has long been used in pastry and confectionary baking. For plant-based cooking, it adds a slightly chewy texture and nutty flavor. A popular brand for almond meal (and for many other specialty flours) is *Bob's Red Mill*. Grocery stores with bulk sections may carry it there or look in the baking section near other gluten-free items.

Bragg Liquid Aminos

This savory, salty liquid can be used as an alternative for any of the recipes calling for soy sauce in this book. Bragg has a similar flavor but uses only non-GMO, unfermented soybeans. If you avoid soy, try coconut aminos instead. (Similarly, if you avoid gluten, use tamari.)

Broth

For the most part, adapting a recipe to a plant-based version is a simple swap of vegetable broth for chicken or beef broth. However there is one product that we feel deserves mention: *Better Than Bouillon*. This is a concentrated stock base that you add to water. It comes in glass jars and can be found with other soup bases and stocks. The "No Chicken" and "No Beef" varieties bring a rich flavor that is a cut above. They also have varieties that contain animal products, so look for the ones that say "Vegetarian" on the label.

Butter, Vegan

The plant-based butter substitute (or technically, "buttery spread") that has long held the top spot is *Earth Balance*. It is available in both tubs and sticks. While it is not an exact taste replica of true butter, it is quite good and can generally be used interchangeably in recipes calling for dairy butter. When veganizing a recipe using *Earth Balance*, pay attention to the total salt content of the dish. *Earth Balance* contains salt.

Cashews, Raw

Nuts might not seem like they need to be included in this list, but cashews in their raw form are used quite often in plant-based cooking. They add a rich creaminess but with less fat and oil than animal-based dairy products. Just be sure to get raw cashews. Purchase them economically in bulk online or in better grocery stores. Cashew pieces are less expensive than whole cashews.

Chickpea Flour

Similar to almond meal, chickpea flour is ground chickpeas (also known as garbanzo beans). Chickpea flour can be used for thickening soups and sauces or to add flavor and texture to plant-based meats. The raw flour has a unique flavor that some consider undesirable, but if it is used in limited quantities, that flavor cooks out. With a high-speed blender you can make your own from dried chickpeas, but for the smoothest consistency, leave the grinding to the professionals! Look for chickpea flour from *Bob's Red Mill*, and in the bulk or gluten-free sections in markets.

Mayonnaise, Vegan

More and more brands of plant-based mayonnaise are showing up on the store shelves lately. The two long-standing favorites are *Just Mayo* and *Vegenaise*. The flavors and textures of the two are distinctly different. Which brand is better depends on personal preference. If you liked *Hellman's* mayonnaise, you will probably prefer *Just Mayo*, but it's worth taste-testing several brands to find your favorite.

Nutritional Yeast

Nutritional yeast is similar to baking yeast in that both are forms of microscopic organisms from the fungi family. However nutritional yeast is "deactivated" with heat. It is yellow and comes either in flakes or powder. For the recipes in this book, use the flakes. Nutritional yeast has a cheesy taste, and is often used in recipes to provide that flavor. Another reason it is popular are its health benefits. "Nooch," as

it is affectionately called, in its natural state is a great source of many B vitamins. When commercially produced it does not contain B12, but the common practice for manufacturers is to fortify it. (This is an important point to verify if you are depending on nutritional yeast for your B12.) In addition, nutritional yeast is a complete protein, having all the essential amino acids. Two tablespoons contains an incredible 9 grams of protein.

Finding nooch in the grocery can be a challenge. Some stores will have it in the bulk section, some in the baking section (look for *Bob's Red Mill*), and still others in the supplements section. Nooch is easily purchased online and often for substantially less cost.

Tahini

Just as peanut butter is made from peanuts, tahini is made from sesame seeds. Tahini has been used in Far and Middle Eastern cuisines for centuries. In plant-based cooking it has become popular as an alternative to peanut butter due to its lower levels of sugar and saturated fats. Tahini can be used to flavor and thicken sauces, dressings and even in baked goods as an oil/fat substitute.

Tapioca Starch

Tapioca starch (also known as tapioca flour) is a thickening agent made from the cassava root. It can be used as a substitute for cornstarch (use 2 tablespoons tapioca starch for 1 tablespoon cornstarch). In Latin countries it is also used in baking for creating a crisp crust. It is a fine white powder, generally found in the baking section. *Bob's Red Mill* carries tapioca starch.

Tempeh

Tofu and tempeh are both made from soybeans. To make tempeh, whole soybeans are fermented and pressed into cake form. It has a slightly nutty, sour flavor. Due to fermentation, tempeh is more easily digested and the nutrients are more readily absorbed. Tempeh is usually sold in a shrink-wrapped package and found in the refrigerated section in the grocery near tofu, miso paste, and meat substitutes.

Some recipes suggest simmering tempeh in water before cooking in order to mellow the flavor and allow it to absorb marinade solutions. We have not found this to be a necessary step. See the **Techniques** section starting on page 20 for a fuss-free way to quickly and easily enjoy tempeh.

Tempeh keeps well in the freezer with no changes to taste or texture after thawing.

Textured Vegetable Protein (TVP)

TVP is another soybean product, although it is a relative newcomer to standard grocery store shelves. It was first developed in the 1960s and could be found at "natural" food markets or co-ops. "TVP" is a registered trademark, so you may also see it labeled as textured soy protein or TSP.

To make TVP, the soy protein is extracted, defatted, and dehydrated. During this process the end product is made into various shapes such as chunks, nuggets, or flakes. The normal process for extracting the soy protein involves chemicals, so if this is a concern to you, look for organic TVP. To use TVP in cooking, first rehydrate it with hot water.

In the grocery TVP is sometimes found in the bulk section. Packaged it is often in the baking section. And you guessed it, *Bob's Red Mill* sells TVP and organic TSP!

Tofu

Tofu is a soybean product that has been around for thousands of years. It is produced by cooking, grinding and straining whole soybeans to make a milk. The milk is then coagulated and pressed into blocks. (This is similar to the process of making cheese from cow's milk.)

There are several different varieties of tofu attained from varying the production process specifics. However for the purposes of this cookbook, there are only two kinds we recommend:

1. Extra-firm tofu: This is the most compact and chewiest of the block tofus. In our experience this is the most versatile as well. In a pinch, firm tofu also works in most recipes. Extra-firm tofu is available in the refrigerated section of the grocery alongside tempeh. Although you can freeze this type of tofu, the resulting texture is tough, almost rubbery, so we don't recommend it.
2. Silken (or soft) tofu: Unlike regular tofu, silken has a dense, smooth consistency. Because of this, it is usually used for sauces and desserts like puddings. Silken tofu is sold in aseptic, shelf-stable packaging, often in the Asian foods aisle.

Tofu by itself has very little flavor. You could eat it raw, but it is not going to taste very good! For almost any application of extra-firm tofu it will need to be pressed. This allows the tofu to absorb flavors added during marinating and cooking. For detailed information on how to press and prepare tofu, see the **Techniques** chapter starting on page 20.

Vital Wheat Gluten

Gluten is made from the protein of wheat. Without gluten, bread would not hold its shape when rising and baking and it wouldn't have that nice chewy yet airy texture we love. In plant-based cooking, gluten is an excellent protein source and an alternative to soy products. When gluten is used in a recipe with broth and flavorings to make a meat substitute, the result is called "seitan" or "wheat meat." Gluten is another product that can be found in bulk sections, or in the baking aisle. *Bob's Red Mill* carries vital wheat gluten and you can also purchase it online.

Worcestershire Sauce, Vegan

How is it that regular Worcestershire sauce is not vegan, you might ask? Because it contains anchovies! That distinctive flavor is difficult to replicate with a do-it-yourself recipe, but there are some good commercially-produced vegan Worcestershire sauce brands, such as *Annie's* and *Wan Ja Shan*.

And finally...the one exception to our "no weird ingredients" rule...

Black Salt

This is one ingredient you will probably not find at your local grocery, and maybe you could say it is a little "weird," or at least amusing! Black salt is not essential to any recipe in this book, but it does take the recipes in which we suggest it up another level. (We have noted where this can be used instead of regular salt in many of the egg alternative recipes.) It is a worthy ingredient to have because it adds an egg-like aroma and taste to food.

Black salt can often be found at Indian or Asian groceries, or online. There are other types of black salt, so don't be confused. You want Indian black salt called *kala namak*. Get the powder form, which is light pink in color. It will have a distinct sulfur smell, but don't be put off by that. It truly enhances the finished product.

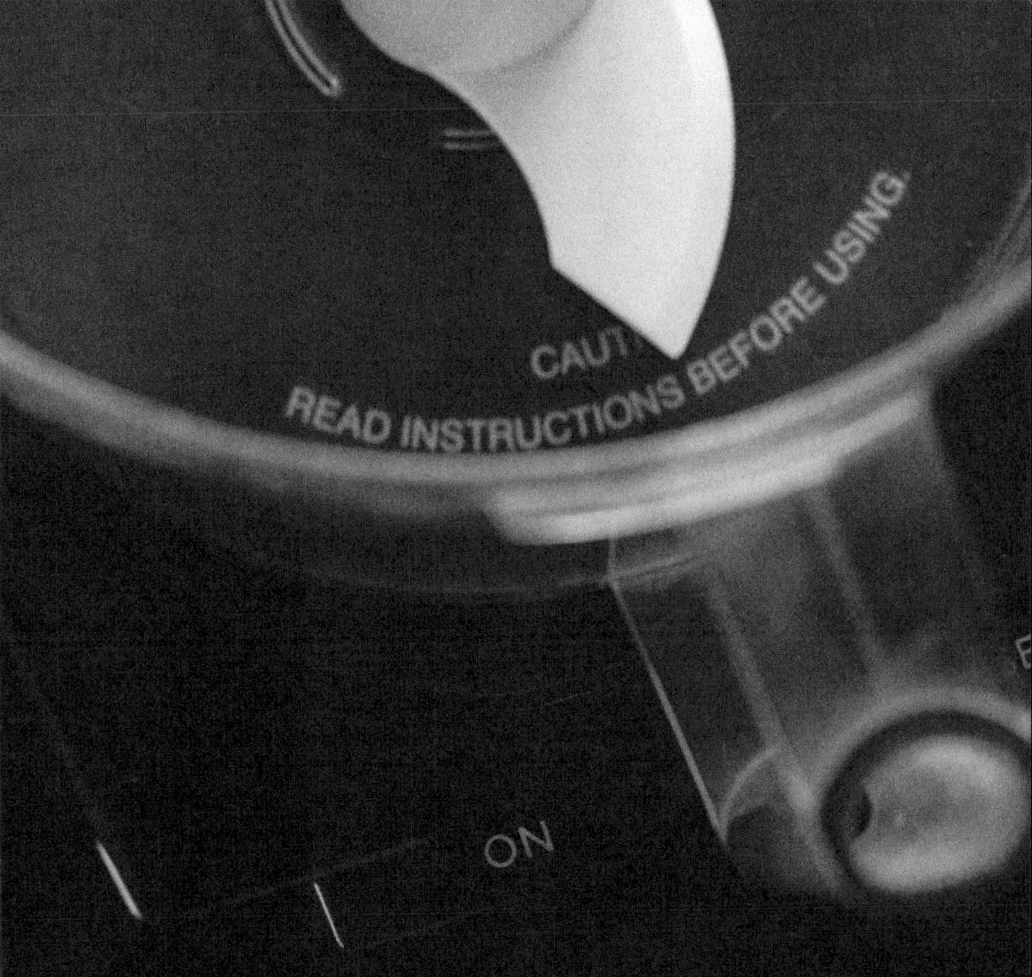

CAUT

READ INSTRUCTIONS BEFORE USING.

ON

Techniques

For the home cook, transitioning to cooking with plant-based meats instead of animal meats requires some adjustments in how food is prepared. Much of this is due to the differences in composition and fat content between plants and animals. We explore and explain those differences in this chapter.

While the individual recipes in this book include tips for preparation, cooking and serving, this section contains helpful pointers for cooking plant-based meats in general. You may find these useful as you venture out on your own – tweaking our recipes, veganizing others, or creating new ones!

Help! Everything is sticking to the pan!

Plant-based meats have a much lower fat content than animal meat which makes them tend to stick to hot cooking surfaces. Therefore, to successfully brown or sear sausages, bacon, burgers, or other plant-based food, you need some techniques on how to keep them from sticking. Coated non-stick pans are fine, but we recommend cast iron skillets. They are extremely useful for everyday cooking and they last forever with proper care. Bonus: a little bit of oil goes a long way in cast iron.

For other pans, such as stainless steel, start out using a drizzle of oil. If the meat continues to stick, rather than add more oil, try deglazing the pan with a few drops of water, vegetable broth, or wine. Deglazing requires some patience and diligence, but it is worth the effort when you think of all the fat that you are avoiding! Plus you get those nice, brown, crunchy bits!

Some plant-based meats will stick more than others.

Some prepared meat alternatives, such as vegan meat crumbles or sausage can be particularly stubborn. Their ingredients and/or small size make them susceptible to sticking and burning quickly. Here, too, adding a little vegetable oil and deglazing with liquid is very effective.

Browning tofu or tempeh in the pan is not too difficult when there's a small quantity of vegetable oil in the pan. You really don't need much for it to be effective.

The veggie burgers look too big.

Again, due to the low fat content, plant-based meats won't shrink as much as animal meats when cooked. In fact, some of the foods will expand if they contain a high quantity of vital wheat gluten, as in seitan. As a general rule, one pound of ground beef will yield 12 ounces of beef after being cooked. So, 12 ounces of vegan beef crumbles is the equivalent of one pound of uncooked ground beef. For veggie burgers, form the patties smaller than you would for ground beef burgers because they will not shrink during frying or baking.

Brown first, set aside, and add near the end.

Many plant-based meat alternatives become more tender - to the point of falling apart - during longer cooking processes. This can be especially true for some of the commercially-prepared meats, like meat crumbles or beefless "tips." As a general rule, if you are adding a meat alternative to a dish, brown it first, remove from the pan and set it aside. Then add it back to the dish near the end of cooking. This is especially helpful with soups and stews.

Are we really trying to replace animal meat, ounce for ounce?

If you are reading this book, chances are good that you believe the answer is NO. The purpose of this cookbook is to highlight the ease and diversity of a vegan diet, and to assist those who are transitioning from a heavily animal meat-based diet into one that is plant-based.

Technically everything in this cookbook is one form or another of a plant, though some of the ingredients are more "processed" (i.e., broken down from their original, whole form, while remaining free of unneeded and unwanted preservatives and additives) than others. We encourage consuming foods that are as close as possible in form as found in nature, making fruits, vegetables, legumes, and grains the centerpiece of each meal rather than placing emphasis on "meat" products. We believe that the standard American diet is skewed too far in the direction of getting meat into every course of every meal.

Why do some recipes simmer seitan while others steam or bake it?

Each of these cooking techniques has advantages and disadvantages. Depending on the dish, one cooking method is preferred over another. This preference was developed over time and with repeated testing and tasting of each seitan recipe in the book. For example, sausages are wrapped in foil and steamed so that the shape is maintained and the finished result is moist and tender.

The traditional method of cooking seitan dishes is to simmer the dough, unwrapped, in a flavored vegetable broth. A properly-simmered seitan is moist and flavorful. But, unless one has a lot of practice with this technique, it can be tricky. If the cooking liquid gets too hot or stays too cool, the seitan can come out with a rubbery texture. Another downside is that the shape of the final product cannot be controlled. Also, the broth is another variable factor that contributes flavors and saltiness to the dough. Finally, there is the issue of what to do with the broth once the seitan is cooked.

While wrapping and steaming the dough is commonly used for sausages and hot dogs, this can also be a quick and easy preparation for loaves and cutlets with the added advantage of retaining moistness. Also, no unanticipated flavors will be added to the seitan during cooking.

Baking is preferred when an outer crust is desired. Wrapping the baking dish in aluminum foil is generally essential to avoid having the seitan dry out during its time in the oven. Baking usually takes longer than steaming, but who doesn't love a nice crust on their brisket? Some recipes even call for first steaming the seitan, then popping it into the oven for a few minutes to achieve a crispy outer crust.

The seitan recipes in this book use the cooking technique that has been found to be the most effective without being too time-consuming, troublesome or difficult to follow.

How can I tell when the seitan is done?
Much like testing a steak for doneness, the same goes for seitan. Press on it with your finger. It should feel firm to the touch - more firm than in its raw state. Or, you can slice into it to see if the center is undercooked. However, once you have prepared a recipe a few times, the required steaming/baking time will become apparent.

Beware of the sticky seitan dough bits!
Mixing up seitan is a lot like working with bread dough. Wet and dry ingredients are combined in a bowl to form a sticky dough. This sticky dough presents a real clean-up challenge! There are those endless, elusive bits that stick to the bowl, utensils, hands – everything! In hot dishwater, they just get gummier and stickier. After making a few batches of seitan the dish sponge is ready for the trash! What to do? There aren't any foolproof, simple techniques we have to offer, unfortunately. But, we have found it helpful to use a bread dough scraper or sturdy spatula to pre-clean the bowl and remove as many of those bits as possible before washing everything in hot water. *The King Arthur Flour* website suggests using cold water to clean rather than warm or hot. The warmer water can further activate and begin to "cook" the sticky gluten.

Tofu and tempeh don't have any flavor.
Some say: "I just don't like the taste of tempeh!" or "Tofu is so bland!" Both of these cooking and nutritional powerhouses have bad reputations – at least in the animal meat-eating world. But, tofu and tempeh are wonderful plant-based meat alternatives – nutritious, versatile and inexpensive – while being minimally processed. They are not meant to be eaten plain, though. They are like sponges that soak up the flavors from sauces, marinades, and seasonings. Before cooking, tofu is usually pressed and drained so that the bland water it is stored in is forced out. It is then ready to better absorb flavorful sauces.

That doesn't mean, though, that enjoying tofu or tempeh equals extra work in the kitchen! Quickly prepare tofu or tempeh by cutting into cubes, placing cubes in a bowl with some soy sauce and tossing to coat. Allow to marinate for at least 30 minutes. Fry the cubes in a pan and add to almost anything – salads, stir fries, curries, and Buddha bowls!

What is the best method for pressing tofu?

If you research online "how to press tofu," you'll find dozens of different methods. Both low-tech and high-tech methods work well, so use what is most convenient for you. No matter which you choose, our tips below give you the whys and hows of pressing tofu to maximize the benefits of this versatile ingredient.

- There are two types of tofu. Refrigerated, water-packed tofu and shelf-stable silken tofu. In this book we primarily use the refrigerated variety.
- For several recipes, we suggest "pressing" the tofu before using it. Pressing squeezes out the flavorless liquid the tofu comes packaged in and "makes room" for marinades and seasonings. It also gives the tofu a firmer texture.
- Tofu should be pressed for at least 30 minutes. The necessity for more time depends on how the tofu will be used. If it will be crumbled, then the minimum time is generally sufficient. If the tofu is to be cubed and sautéed, press for an hour. If the tofu is going to be sliced thinly, then a denser, firmer texture is better, so plan on 2+ hours, or even as long as overnight.
- Tofu consistency makes a difference. Not all extra-firm tofu brands are the same. Some are denser than others and come wrapped tightly in plastic with only a small amount of water. This variety needs minimal or even no pressing.
- If you use tofu frequently, you may wish to invest in a tofu press. Presses efficiently extract the liquid without crushing or damaging the tofu. There are several designs, so do some research before purchasing. They aren't cheap!
- For pressing without a dedicated gadget, invert a smooth-bottomed plate in the sink, place the block of tofu on the plate and place another plate on top. Weigh the top plate down with a cast iron skillet or some other heavy object. Make sure to place the weight evenly so that one end of the tofu does not get crushed.

To process or not to process; that is the question.

Blenders and food processors are used frequently when making plant-based meats and cheeses and using them to ease recipe prep can become quite addictive. They are like the electric power tools of the kitchen. It is easy to get carried away: throw everything in there, hit the button, and fall under the spell of the spinning blades! Before you know it, instead of a rough *chop* you have a silky *puree*. Or, items that were meant to be stirred in by hand to provide a concentrated "bite" become melded with all the other ingredients.

The recipes in this book provide instructions on which order to mix ingredients together and when there can be a risk of over-processing. If you are customizing a recipe or creating your own, however, do keep the textures and flavors of the finished product in mind before you hit the On button!

Pay attention to other sources of salt in the recipes.
Everyone's taste for salt is different. That is why our recipes have *suggested* measures for salt. It is up to the home cook to decide how much or how little should be added. Also, be aware that other ingredients such as soy sauce, tamari, liquid aminos, vegetable broth, liquid smoke, canned beans, etc., can contribute to the level of saltiness. Taste first, then season. As you've probably heard many times, it is much simpler to add salt to a dish than to remove it!

Another consideration is that as you transition to more plant-based eating, your taste buds will become more sensitive to salts, sweets, and fats. You may notice a difference after just a few weeks. What seems "just right" today can quickly become too salty, sweet, or fatty! So, keep this in mind as you prepare your food. And - get ready to discover and enjoy the true, delicious flavors of plants!

Tools & Equipment

The beauty of the recipes in this book is that they don't require a lot of tools or expensive equipment to make, and you probably already have most of these items in your kitchen! Beyond the requisite knives (good, sharp ones, of course!), mixing bowls, baking sheets, spoons, and pots and pans, below are some additional tools that will help in preparing our recipes.

Cutting Board

A good cutting board or two is a must. Wood or renewable bamboo is preferable because they are germ-resistant, but plastic will also work. Avoid glass cutting boards as they can dull and damage a knife's edge.

Vegetable Peeler

A peeler that fits comfortably in your hand makes quick work of removing the skins from beets, potatoes, and carrots.

Food Processor

We just can't do without one of these! A food processor quickly mixes ingredients, and with the proper attachments (included with most units) you can also easily shred and slice. If you only have a smaller-sized food processor or food prep machine, work in batches to ensure even chopping and mixing.

Blender

Don't worry if you don't have one of those fancy high-speed blenders. A regular blender will work just fine for the recipes in this book, but you may need to blend longer to get the desired consistency.

Steamer Basket

Some of our seitan-based recipes require steaming to cook. If you already have a steamer, yay! If not, you may wish to invest in a bamboo steamer, or find an inexpensive, adjustable metal steamer basket that fits into a large, deep pot. Most kitchen stores and even *Target* and *Walmart* carry these handy metal steamer baskets.

Cast Iron Skillet

Invest in a cast iron skillet or two and they could very well become family heirlooms passed down from one generation to the next. Cast iron pans and pots are incredibly durable and they're ideal for cooking everything from scrambled tofu to tempeh bacon to veggie burgers – because with only a thin slick of oil, they become non-stick. A 10-inch skillet is nice and roomy and it's heavy enough to double as a tofu press. We love kitchen multi-taskers!

Large Pot with Lid
You'll need a deep, lidded pot for steaming or boiling.

Grater
A box grater works well to shred vegetables. They're especially handy if you don't need a quantity large enough to justify getting your food processor dirty!

Aluminum Foil and Parchment Paper
In this book we use aluminum foil to shape and wrap sausages prior to cooking and to cover baking sheets. Parchment paper can also be used in the sausage-making process, and it makes a great liner for baking sheets when you don't want or need to use oil to keep food from sticking.

Silicone Baking Sheets
Silicone baking sheet liners are a great "green" way to bake not only because they are washable and reusable, but also because you don't need to add oil to the surface. Veggie burgers and sausage patties (not to mention cookies!) can be removed with ease. Durable and long-lasting, pick up one or two at kitchen stores or online.

Mortar and Pestle
This isn't a must-have item, but it is extremely efficient when crushing a small quantity of herbs and seeds.

Recipes

Main Course Meats

Seitan BBQ Brisket
Seitan Cutlets
Lentil Meatloaf
Italian Meatballs
TVP Ground Beef
Tempeh Sausage Crumbles
Artichoke Crab Cakes
Sofritas
Tofu Teriyaki Strips

Seitan BBQ Brisket

This flavorful brisket will please vegans and non-vegans alike. Everyone who has tried it is amazed at how good it is! **Serves 6**

Ingredients

2 ½ cups vital wheat gluten
1 ½ cups whole wheat flour
1 tablespoon garlic powder
1 tablespoon onion powder
1 teaspoon ground black pepper
1 teaspoon smoked paprika
1 teaspoon chili powder
1/3 cup olive oil
1/3 cup low-sodium soy sauce
2 ½ tablespoons tahini
2 ½ tablespoons barbecue sauce, plus more for topping and serving
1 tablespoon liquid smoke
1 cup low-sodium vegetable broth

Directions

Preheat oven to 350-degrees F and line an 8-inch x 11-inch baking pan with foil. Leave one side of the foil long to wrap the brisket.

In a medium-sized bowl, mix together the dry ingredients. In a small bowl, whisk together the wet ingredients. Add the wet mixture to the dry and stir to form a dough, then knead for about 5 minutes. Let the dough rest for 20 minutes to make the brisket easier to form.

Shape dough into a 5-inch x 10-inch rectangle. Pour some barbecue sauce onto the bottom of the foil-lined pan and place the brisket on top of the sauce. Spread more sauce on top of the brisket and seal tightly with the extra foil. Bake for 1 hour.

Slice and serve with additional barbecue sauce, if desired.

Tips/Techniques/Substitutions

- To give the brisket more texture, after shaping the dough into a rectangle, cut it into thick slabs. Then press the slabs together and place into the foil-lined pan.
- The brisket can be baked without wrapping in foil, but do cover the pan with foil. Bake for 30 minutes, then flip the brisket over and bake for another 30 minutes or until cooked throughout.

Final Preparation & Serving Suggestions

- Cut into thick slices and serve with coleslaw and potato salad.
- Cut into thin slices and make a sandwich with pickles and onions.

Seitan
BBQ
Brisket

Seitan
Cutlets

Seitan Cutlets

These flavorful seitan cutlets are extremely easy to prepare. One bite and you will realize that they are also quite versatile as a substitute for chicken in just about any recipe. As they say in a popular Tulsa restaurant, "Hello, chicken fry!" **Serves 8**

Ingredients

1 15-ounce can white beans, rinsed and drained
1 cup water
1 tablespoon olive oil
1 tablespoon fresh lemon juice
2 cups vital wheat gluten
$\frac{1}{2}$ cup chickpea flour
$\frac{1}{4}$ cup nutritional yeast
2 teaspoons onion powder
1 teaspoon poultry seasoning
1 teaspoon garlic powder
$\frac{3}{4}$ teaspoon ground celery seed
$\frac{1}{4}$ teaspoon salt
2 cups vegan chicken-style broth

Directions

Preheat oven to 300-degrees F and set aside two 9-inch x 13-inch glass or ceramic baking pans.

Process the beans and $\frac{1}{2}$ cup water in a food processor until smooth. Small chunks are fine as they add to the texture of the cutlets. Add the lemon juice, oil and the remaining water and pulse to mix well.

In a separate bowl, combine the dry ingredients. Pour in the bean mixture and stir until a soft dough forms. Taste for salt and adjust as needed. The dough should be slightly less salty than what you want for the cooked cutlets. (During cooking, the cutlets will absorb additional flavor and salt from the broth.) Knead dough for 4–5 minutes by hand or in a stand mixer.

Divide into 8 pieces and flatten into $\frac{1}{2}$-inch to $\frac{3}{4}$-inch thick cutlets, depending on how they will be served. Lightly oil the bottoms of the two baking dishes and divide the broth between the pans. Place the cutlets in the pans and cover with aluminum foil. Bake for 30 minutes. Flip the cutlets over and cook for another 15–30 minutes. Most of the broth should be absorbed by the time the cutlets are done.

Tips/Techniques/Substitutions

- Balancing the salt content is one of the most important aspects of this recipe. Added salt can come from the beans and the broth.
- When tasting the raw dough you might detect a bitter flavor from the chickpea flour. This cooks out during baking.
- If the dough keeps "springing back" while forming into cutlets, let it rest for a few minutes, then flatten and reshape.
- Baking the cutlets in broth results in a moist, tender meat that is very versatile. However, you can also form the dough into logs, wrap in foil and steam for 40 minutes and then bake at 350-degrees F for 10–20 minutes for a very nice roasted crust on the outside.
- During baking the cutlets may adhere to the bottom of the pan. When you flip them over, use a spatula to separate them cleanly from the pan.

Final Preparation & Serving Suggestions

- Slice or cube and pan fry to sprinkle on top of salads.
- Stir into soups and stews.
- Slice thin for sandwiches.
- Dice and toss with hot sauce, then pan fry for buffalo flavor!
- Bread and fry the cutlets or sear on the grill.
- Thinly slice and fold into fajitas, enchiladas, tacos, or add to stir-frys.

Lentil Meatloaf

Let's be honest. Meatloaf is never going to win any beauty contests, but when you combine all these flavorful, whole food ingredients, slather them with tangy barbecue sauce and bake, you will be amazed at how mouthwatering it looks and – even better – how delicious it tastes!
Serves 6-8

Ingredients

1 cup brown lentils, picked over and rinsed
2 cups water
1 14-ounce package extra-firm tofu, pressed and drained
4 celery stalks, chopped
½ yellow onion, chopped
2 garlic cloves, minced
¼ cup walnuts, finely ground
1 ¼ cup quick cooking oats (see Tips)
3 tablespoons low-sodium soy sauce
1 tablespoon steak sauce, such as *A1*
1 tablespoon ketchup
1 tablespoon Dijon mustard
2 teaspoons dried parsley
½ teaspoon dried rubbed sage
½ teaspoon dried rosemary
½ teaspoon dried thyme

Directions

Place the lentils in a medium-sized saucepan and cover with the 2 cups of water. Cook for about 40 minutes, or until tender. Drain any excess water. Set aside.

While the lentils cook, mash the tofu in a large mixing bowl using a potato masher or your hands. Add the cooked lentils to the tofu and mash again, leaving some texture.

Lightly oil a 9-inch x 5-inch loaf pan and preheat the oven to 350-degrees F.

In a small skillet over medium heat, sauté the onion and celery in oil until soft. Add the garlic and cook an additional 30 seconds. Remove skillet from heat and let cool slightly before adding to the tofu-lentil mixture. Stir in the remaining ingredients. Taste and adjust seasonings.

Press the tofu-lentil mixture firmly into the prepared pan. Bake for 50–60 minutes.

Tips/Techniques/Substitutions

- Rolled oats can easily be made into quick-cooking oats by pulsing them in a food processor until crumbly.
- If desired, you can spread some barbecue sauce on top prior to baking for a nice glaze.
- The meatloaf can be baked in a large-sized 6-muffin pan. The bake time is about half – 30 minutes.

Final Preparation & Serving Suggestions

- Serve with mashed potatoes and gravy.
- Make a meatloaf sandwich.
- Serve with additional barbecue sauce on the side.

Lentil
Meatloaf

Italian
Meatballs

Italian Meatballs

You'll enjoy making these meatballs because you don't have to fry them. Just mix them up, form and bake in the oven. **Makes 16 meatballs**

Ingredients

½ cup yellow onion, finely chopped
½ cup carrot, finely chopped
2 garlic cloves, minced
½ cup walnuts
1 14-ounce package extra-firm tofu, pressed and drained
1 cup cooked short grain brown rice
2 tablespoons dried parsley, or ¼ cup fresh, chopped
½ cup bread crumbs (dry or fresh)
2 tablespoons nutritional yeast
1 teaspoon dried thyme
1 teaspoon salt
1 teaspoon dried basil
1 tablespoon low-sodium soy sauce
1 tablespoon fresh lemon juice
1 tablespoon steak sauce, such as *A1*
dash of red pepper flakes, optional
2–3 tablespoons vital wheat gluten, optional

Directions

Sauté the onion and carrot in vegetable oil over medium-high heat until soft, about 7 minutes. Stir in the garlic and cook for 30 seconds. Remove vegetables from the heat and place in a bowl.

Pulse the walnuts in a food processor until crumbled. (Do not over process or they will turn into walnut butter.) Transfer to the bowl with the onion mixture.

Pulse the tofu in the food processor until smooth. Add the rice and pulse a few times to mix. Transfer to the bowl and stir in the remaining ingredients. Mix well. The dough will be tacky, but not so sticky that you cannot form balls. If desired, refrigerate the mixture for an hour or more to make the meatballs easier to shape.

Roll into about sixteen balls. Place meatballs on a silicone sheet or on a lightly oiled baking sheet. When ready to cook, preheat the oven to 350-degrees F. Bake for 20 minutes. Turn meatballs over and bake 20–25 minutes more, or until browned. (The suggested cooking time is for meatballs that are about 2" in diameter. Smaller meatballs require less cooking time.)

Tips/Techniques/Substitutions

- The vital wheat gluten is optional, but it helps to hold the meatballs to-gether.
- We recommend using short grain brown rice because it is stickier than long grain rice and helps to hold the meatballs together. You can use any other rice, but the meatballs might be more delicate.
- Give the walnuts a quick chop by hand before adding them to the food processor. This helps to get an even crumble. Also, sort through the wal-nuts prior to processing as on occasion there might be pieces of the hard interior partition of the shell. They are not fun to bite down on and can damage teeth!
- As an alternative to baking, fry meatballs in vegetable or olive oil for a really crispy crust.

Final Preparation & Serving Suggestions

- These are ideal for that classic family favorite – meatballs and spaghetti.
- Serve on a toasted bun with marinara sauce and melted vegan cheese for a meatball sub.
- Crumble the meatballs for a delicious salad topper.
- Stir into Italian-style soups, such as Wedding Soup.

TVP Ground Beef

Frozen plant-based burger crumbles are available at supermarkets, but making your own at home is easy, healthier and much less expensive. **Makes about 12 ounces**

Ingredients

1 cup low-sodium vegetable broth
1 cup Textured Vegetable Protein (TVP)
2 tablespoons low-sodium soy sauce
1 tablespoon steak sauce, such as *A1*
½ teaspoon onion powder
½ teaspoon garlic powder
1 tablespoon vegetable oil

Directions

In a microwave, heat the vegetable broth to a boil in a small, heat-resistant bowl and stir in the TVP. Add the remaining ingredients, except for the oil. Cover and let sit for 10 minutes.

Heat the oil in a non-stick or cast iron skillet over medium-high heat. Transfer the mixture to the pan and flatten with a spatula so that it resembles a pancake.

When the first side is browned, after about 5 minutes, carefully flip to brown the other side. Add more oil if needed. When the other side is browned, about 5 more minutes, break up TVP with a spatula to create chunks. Cook for a few more minutes for even browning.

Use immediately in your favorite recipes that call for ground beef, or store in an air-tight container in the refrigerator until ready to use.

Tips/Techniques/Substitutions

* This recipe is equivalent to about 1 pound of cooked ground beef.

Final Preparation & Serving Suggestions

* Mix in some chili powder and/or cumin (or use a taco seasoning mix), for a quick taco or burrito filling.
* Add to marinara sauces and stir into spaghetti.
* Use as a replacement for ground beef in casseroles.

Tempeh Sausage Crumbles

Tempeh may look odd, but it is packed with nutrition and unlike bland tofu has a pleasant earthy, mushroom-like flavor. Combined with the typical spices and herbs used in traditional sausage, the end result is a plant-based alternative that is a snap to prepare. **Makes about 1 1/2 cups**

Ingredients

1 8-ounce package tempeh, crumbled
1 tablespoon low-sodium soy sauce
½ teaspoon fennel seed, crushed
¼ teaspoon dried basil
¼ teaspoon dried oregano
¼ teaspoon dried sage
2 garlic cloves, finely minced
½ teaspoon fresh lemon juice

Directions

Crumble the tempeh into a small bowl and stir in the soy sauce to evenly distribute. Let tempeh sit for at least 30 minutes to allow it to absorb the sauce. Stir in the remaining ingredients.

Sauté tempeh in vegetable oil in a skillet over medium-high heat. Cook until browned, about 10 minutes.

Tips/Techniques/Substitutions

• Use a splatter screen when sautéing the tempeh crumbles. When the pieces get hot, they can pop right out of the pan!

Final Preparation & Serving Suggestions

• Top a pizza with the crumbles.
• Fold into *Tofu Egg Cakes* (page 102) or *Tofu Scrambled Egg* (page 104).
• Make a breakfast burrito with the crumbles and sautéed vegetables.

Artichoke Crab Cakes

These cakes are so delicious you will want to serve them for parties and dinners with friends. Paired with a creamy remoulade sauce no one will believe these are 100% plant-based! **Makes 8-10 cakes**

Ingredients

1 ½ cups *Ritz* crackers, crushed
1 15-ounce can artichoke hearts, rinsed and drained
1 15-ounce can hearts of palm, rinsed and drained
3 scallions, chopped
¼ cup red bell pepper, seeded and diced
¼ cup corn (fresh or frozen that has been thawed)
¼ cup celery, diced
2 teaspoons *Old Bay Seasoning*
½ teaspoon garlic powder
1 teaspoon dried parsley
1/8 teaspoon crushed/powdered dried thyme
3 tablespoons vegan mayonnaise

Directions

In the bowl of a food processor, pulse the crackers to the consistency of coarse flour. Transfer to a small bowl and set aside.

Add the artichokes and hearts of palm to the bowl of the food processor and process until chunky. Add scallions, red bell pepper, corn and celery and pulse to combine. Transfer to a large bowl and stir in the seasonings and mayonnaise. Mix in one cup of the cracker crumbs.

Shape into small patties, about 2 tablespoons per cake. Lightly coat patties in remaining cracker crumbs. Pan fry in vegetable oil over medium-high heat, 2–3 minutes per side, or until golden brown.

Tips/Techniques/Substitutions

* If you cook the patties in two batches, be sure to wipe out the pan between batches to remove any crumbs, as they will burn.
* Chilling the mixture in the refrigerator for an hour will make these moist patties easier to form.

Final Preparation & Serving Suggestions

* Serve as an appetizer with a remoulade or spicy red pepper sauce.
* Serve alongside fresh cabbage or veggie slaw.

Sofritas

In traditional Latin American cooking, sofritas are a spicy blend of cooked garlic, peppers, onions, and tomatoes. This flavorful mix can also be used to enhance other dishes. *Chipotle's* restaurant chain offers tofu sofritas in their bowls and burritos. Unfortunately, their version can sometimes taste too heavily seasoned. Make your own at home and season it the way you like it! **Makes about 1 1/2 cups**

Ingredients

1 14-ounce package extra-firm tofu, pressed and drained
1 tablespoon low-sodium soy sauce
2 teaspoons dried oregano
¾ teaspoon ground cumin
½ teaspoon ground coriander
½ teaspoon sugar
1 poblano chile, roasted (see Tips)
½ small onion, diced
2 garlic cloves, minced
½ cup low-sodium vegetable broth
1 ½ tablespoons tomato paste
1–2 teaspoons chipotle in adobo sauce
1 tablespoon apple cider vinegar

Directions

Slice the tofu into small cubes and place in a bowl. Sprinkle with soy sauce, stir, and let sit for 5–10 minutes.

In a skillet over medium-high heat, brown tofu in some vegetable oil. Remove from the pan and roughly chop. Return the cubes to the pan, stir in the oregano, cumin, coriander and sugar and continue to sauté for about 2 minutes.

Meanwhile, in the bowl of a food processor, puree the poblano, onion, garlic, broth, tomato paste, chipotle in adobo and vinegar. Pour the sauce into the pan and stir to coat cubes. Cover pan and cook for 5–7 minutes or until most of the liquid has been absorbed.

Tips/Techniques/Substitutions

* Roast the poblano by slicing in half, removing the seeds and membranes and then placing pieces on a baking sheet under a broiler for 2–3 minutes. Watch closely! Place pieces in a small bowl, cover and let sit for about 10 minutes so that the skin loosens, making removal easier. Discard skins.
* Turn up the heat by adding cayenne or chili powder.

Final Preparation & Serving Suggestions

* Sprinkle sofritas on top of a salad.
* Use sofritas as a filling for a taco or burrito.

Sofritas

Tofu
Teriyaki
Strips

Tofu Teriyaki Strips

With just the right amount of chew, you won't play "tug-of-war" with this jerky when you bite into it! Ideal for snacking, one batch costs just a little more than the price for a tub of tofu! **Serves 6**

Ingredients

1 14-ounce package extra-firm tofu, pressed overnight and drained
½ cup teriyaki sauce, plus more for brushing on top
½ cup canned pinto beans, rinsed and drained
2 teaspoons vegetable oil
1 teaspoon liquid smoke
1-inch chunk fresh ginger, peeled and grated
2 cloves garlic, chopped
1½ teaspoons onion flakes
1 teaspoon garlic powder
1 teaspoon ground black pepper
¾ cup vital wheat gluten
½ tablespoon sesame seeds, for sprinkling on top

Directions

Preheat the oven to 350-degrees F and line a baking sheet with a silicone mat or parchment paper. Set aside two large lengths of plastic wrap that are several inches longer than the baking sheet.

Crumble tofu into the bowl of a food processor and add the ½ cup teriyaki sauce, pinto beans, vegetable oil, liquid smoke, ginger, garlic, onion flakes, garlic powder and black pepper. Process until the tofu is smooth, scraping down the sides of the bowl once or twice. Add the vital wheat gluten and process until the dough forms a ball. Taste and adjust the seasonings.

Scrape mixture onto the center of the baking sheet and form the dough into a thick rectangle. Drape the two sheets of plastic wrap, overlapping them a little, to completely cover the rectangle of dough. Using a rolling pin, roll out the dough until it nearly covers the baking sheet. It should be about ¼-inch thick, but don't worry about the thickness being even as this will give the jerky strips texture.

Remove the plastic wrap. Using the back of a fork, swirl and press into the dough to create ridges for a "meaty" look. With a knife or pizza cutter, divide the dough lengthwise into 6–8 strips, then cut widthwise into ~5" pieces. Brush the top of the dough with teriyaki sauce and sprinkle with sesame seeds.

Bake for 35–40 minutes, checking after about 30 minutes to make sure the edges aren't browning too quickly. If the strips along the edges are crisping too much, remove them from the pan and return the remainder to the oven.

Let strips cool completely before re-cutting and separating the pieces. Store jerky in an air-tight container in the refrigerator.

Tips/Techniques/Substitutions

- Press the tofu for at least 8 hours to remove as much liquid as possible.
- The texture of the strips is best after setting overnight in the refrigerator.
- Divide the dough between two baking sheets if you have difficulty fitting it all onto one pan.
- Add a spicy kick with a dash of red pepper flakes or cayenne pepper.
- Omit the ginger and substitute barbecue sauce for the teriyaki sauce.

Sausages

Seitan Artichoke and Spinach Sausages
Seitan Italian Sausages
Seitan Aloha Sausages
Seitan Andouille Sausages

Seitan Artichoke and Spinach Sausages

You can't go wrong when you make something with both artichokes and spinach in it! They are a winning flavor combination, and these sausages are further proof of that. **Serves 5**

Ingredients

½ cup cooked white beans, rinsed and drained
1 cup vegan chicken-style broth or low-sodium vegetable broth
1 tablespoon olive oil
2 tablespoons low-sodium soy sauce
½ cup canned, water-packed artichoke hearts, drained well and roughly chopped
½ cup fresh spinach, roughly chopped
2 tablespoons fresh lemon juice
2 garlic cloves, minced
1 ¼ –1 ¾ cups vital wheat gluten
¼ cup nutritional yeast
1 teaspoon ground black pepper
¾ teaspoon salt
½ teaspoon rubbed sage

Directions

Tear off five pieces of aluminum foil that measure approximately 6-inches x 12-inches each for forming the sausages. Set aside. Place a steamer basket in a large pot with enough water to just reach the bottom of the basket, but don't heat the water just yet.

In a large bowl, mash beans until no whole ones remain. Add the remaining ingredients and mix thoroughly using a fork or your hands.

Divide mixture into 5 equal portions and shape each into an approximately 5" sausage. To wrap, place one portion near the bottom of the long side of a piece of aluminum foil and roll, allowing some room for the sausages to expand as they cook. Twist the ends to close – like a Tootsie Roll. Repeat with the remaining portions.

Bring the water in the pot to a boil, then turn down the heat to a simmer. Place foil-wrapped sausages in the steamer basket, cover pot and cook sausages for 40–45 minutes.

Let cool long enough to handle before unwrapping and using. Serve immediately or store sausages in an air-tight container in the refrigerator until ready to use.

Tips/Techniques/Substitutions

- Great Northern, navy, or cannellini beans all work well in this recipe.
- For this recipe it is very important to drain the artichokes and squeeze as much moisture out of them as possible, otherwise the dough will be too wet.

Final Preparation & Serving Suggestions

- These are delicious sliced and sautéed in olive oil, then tossed with pasta and your preferred sauce.

Seitan
Artichoke
and
Spinach
Sausages

Seitan
Italian
Sausages

Seitan Italian Sausages

Don't be deterred by the long list of ingredients - most of which are seasonings. Making your own plant-based sausages is actually quite simple and does not require special equipment, other than an inexpensive steamer basket. **Serves 5-6**

Ingredients

1 ½ cups vital wheat gluten
¼ cup whole wheat flour
2 tablespoons nutritional yeast
1 ½ tablespoons brown sugar
3 teaspoons fennel seeds, crushed
2 teaspoons ground black pepper
1 ½ teaspoons dried thyme
1 ½ teaspoons dried oregano
1 ½ teaspoons onion powder
1 teaspoon ground coriander
1 teaspoon smoked paprika
½ teaspoon salt
4 ounces extra-firm tofu, drained and pressed
1 cup low-sodium vegetable broth
¼ cup olive oil
2 tablespoons low-sodium soy sauce
1 ½ tablespoons tomato paste
2–3 cloves garlic, minced

Directions

Preheat oven to 350-degrees F. Tear off five or six, 6-inch x 12-inch pieces of aluminum foil for wrapping the sausages. Set aside.

In a large bowl whisk together the vital wheat gluten, whole wheat flour, nutritional yeast, brown sugar and spices.

Place the tofu, vegetable broth, olive oil, soy sauce, tomato paste and garlic in the bowl of a food processor or blender and pulse until smooth.

Add the wet ingredients to the dry and knead for several minutes until thoroughly combined. Divide dough into 5 or 6 pieces and form each piece into a sausage shape. Place sausages near the long side of the foil sheets. Roll up and twist the ends, leaving some room for the sausages to expand as they cook. Place sausages seam side down on a baking sheet and bake for 30–40 minutes, or until they are firm to the touch.

Let cool slightly before unwrapping and using. Serve immediately or store sausages in an air-tight container in the refrigerator until ready to use.

Final Preparation & Serving Suggestions

- Slice, sauté in a bit of olive oil and add to your favorite pasta sauce.
- Grill and serve in a toasted bun with sautéed onions and peppers. Top with marinara and shredded vegan mozzarella.

Seitan Aloha Sausages

You might notice that this recipe and the *Seitan Artichoke and Spinach Sausages* (page 58) recipe are similar in that both use beans, broth, gluten and nutritional yeast as a base. The differences are in the seasonings and add-ins. This is a great example of taking a basic recipe and making it your own, using past experiences and personal tastes for inspiration, such as a vacation to Hawaii! **Serves 6**

Ingredients

½ cup cooked Great Northern or navy beans, rinsed and drained
1 cup vegan chicken-style broth
1 tablespoon olive oil
2 tablespoons low-sodium soy sauce
2 tablespoons teriyaki sauce
½ cup finely chopped pineapple
¼ cup toasted chopped macadamia nuts
1 teaspoon salt
1 teaspoon ground ginger
1 teaspoon turmeric
1 ¼ –1 ¾ cups vital wheat gluten
¼ cup nutritional yeast

Directions

Tear off six, 6-inch x 12-inch pieces of aluminum foil for wrapping the sausages. Place a steamer basket in a large pot with enough water to just reach the bottom of the basket, but don't heat the water just yet.

In a large bowl, mash beans until no whole ones are left. Add the rest of the ingredients in order listed and mix with a fork. Divide into 6 equal parts. Shape each into a 5" sausage. Wrap sausages in aluminum foil, allowing some room for them to expand as they cook. Twist the ends closed.

Bring the water in the pot to a boil, then turn down the heat to a simmer. Place foil-wrapped sausages in the steamer basket, cover pot and cook for 40–45 minutes.

Let cool long enough to handle before unwrapping and using. Serve immediately or store sausages in an air-tight container in the refrigerator until ready to use.

Seitan Andouille Sausages

There are some classic Cajun dishes for which you must have the smoky, spicy, earthy flavor of andouille sausage. This recipe fits the bill nicely.
Serves 6

Ingredients

½ cup cooked red beans, rinsed and drained if using canned
1 cup low-sodium vegetable broth
2 tablespoons low-sodium soy sauce
1 tablespoon olive oil
4 teaspoons liquid smoke
3 tablespoons finely chopped green bell pepper
2 tablespoons minced garlic
3 teaspoons ground black pepper
3 teaspoons paprika
2 teaspoons onion powder
1 teaspoon chili powder
¾ teaspoon salt
½ teaspoon dried thyme
½ teaspoon ground cumin
¼ teaspoon mace
¼ teaspoon crushed red pepper
¼ teaspoon cayenne pepper
1 ¼ –1 ¾ cups vital wheat gluten
2 tablespoons nutritional yeast

Directions

Tear off six, 6-inch x 12-inch pieces of aluminum foil for wrapping the sausages. Set aside. Place a steamer basket in a large pot with enough water to just reach the bottom of the basket, but don't heat the water just yet.

In a large bowl, mash beans until no whole ones remain. Add the rest of the ingredients in order listed and mix with a fork. Divide mixture into six equal pieces. Shape each into a 5" sausage. Wrap sausages in aluminum foil, allowing some room for them to expand during cooking. Twist the ends closed.

Bring the water in the pot to a boil, then turn down the heat to a simmer. Place foil-wrapped sausages in the steamer basket, cover pot and cook for 40–45 minutes.

Let cool slightly before unwrapping and using. Serve immediately or store sausages in an air-tight container in the refrigerator until ready to use.

Tips/Techniques/Substitutions

- Do not use kidney beans for this recipe. The skins are too tough and do not break down adequately.

Final Preparation & Serving Suggestions

- Slice sausages and stir into vegan jambalaya.
- Serve these sausages in or alongside vegan gumbo or red beans and rice.
- These taste great grilled and tucked into a hot dog bun.

Photos of Seitan Andouille Sausages on pages 68-69.

Burgers
&
Sandwiches

Black Bean Burgers
Old-Fashioned Burgers
Curried Lentil Burgers
Seitan Tofu Bologna
Portobello Mushroom Burgers
Chickpea Tuna Fish
Tofu Tawook
TVP Ham Salad
Tofu Hot Dogs

Black Bean Burgers

This classic veggie burger features black beans, corn and rice and has been tweaked over the years to delicious perfection. The recipes that inspired this one included sweet ingredients like ketchup which just didn't work well with the additional sweetness from the corn and red onion. All it took was eliminating the ketchup and adding Dijon mustard...*Bingo!*

Makes 8-9 patties

Ingredients

1 cup red onion, chopped
1 garlic clove, minced
1 cup cooked short grain brown rice
1 15-ounce can black beans, rinsed and drained
1 cup cooked corn
2 tablespoons Dijon mustard
1 teaspoon ground cumin
$\frac{1}{4}$ teaspoon salt
3 tablespoons vital wheat gluten
$\frac{1}{2}$ –$\frac{3}{4}$ cup bread crumbs

Directions

In a small skillet over medium heat, sauté the onion in vegetable oil until soft and browned, 6–8 minutes. Add the garlic and cook for about 30 seconds. Remove pan from the heat.

Pulse the beans, rice, corn, mustard, cumin, salt and vital wheat gluten in the bowl of a food processor, being sure to leave some texture. Scrape mixture into a medium-sized bowl.

Stir in the onions and enough breadcrumbs to get a slightly tacky mixture. Taste for seasoning and add more salt, if needed. Refrigerate for at least one hour.

Form into 8–9 patties and brown in a lightly oiled skillet over medium heat. Cook 4–5 minutes on each side.

Tips/Techniques/Substitutions

- We recommend using short grain brown rice because it's stickier than long grain rice and helps to hold the burgers together. You can use any other type of rice, but the burgers might not hold together as well.
- You can grill the burgers, but we recommend frying them first so that an outer crust forms.
- These can be baked rather than fried, but the crust will not be as crispy.
- Mix in some chopped jalapeños to spice these up. They can add moisture so stir in more bread crumbs, if needed.

Final Preparation & Serving Suggestions

- These burgers are so flavorful on their own there's no need for condiments, but a smear of chipotle "mayo," with some lettuce and tomato is delicious.
- Wrap the burger in a tortilla with some avocado slices, lettuce and hummus.
- Top a salad with chopped burger.

Black
Bean
Burgers

Old-
Fashioned
Burgers

Old-Fashioned Burgers

The truth is, much of the appeal of a beef burger is in the condiments and fixings. The actual burger patty itself does not have a lot of flavor compared to veggie burgers. When you want to let the flavor of the condiments shine, this is the ideal burger. **Makes 8 patties**

Ingredients

½ cup short grain brown rice
I cup brown lentils, picked over and rinsed
½ yellow onion, chopped
2 garlic cloves, minced
I cup walnuts, chopped
2 teaspoons steak sauce, such as A I
2 teaspoons wet yellow mustard
½ teaspoon salt
½ –¾ cup dry bread crumbs
3 tablespoons vital wheat gluten, optional

Directions

Put the rice into a pot with 3 cups of water. Bring to a boil and lower heat to a simmer. Cover pot and cook for 10 minutes. Stir in the lentils and continue cooking, covered, for an additional 25–35 minutes, or until lentils and rice are tender. Remove from the heat, uncover, and let cool slightly.

In a saucepan, sauté the onion until soft and browned. Add the garlic and cook 30 seconds. Remove from heat. Transfer to a large bowl.

While the rice and lentils are cooking, pulse the walnuts in a food processor until crumbled. (Do not over process or they will turn into walnut butter.) Transfer to the bowl with the onion.

Scrape the lentils and rice into the food processor and pulse a few times. Do not puree. Whole and chopped pieces of lentils and rice add texture to the burgers. Transfer to the bowl with the onion and mix in the remaining ingredients. Taste and adjust seasoning as needed.

The dough should be tacky, but not so sticky that you cannot form the burgers. If desired, refrigerate the mixture for an hour or more to make the dough easier to handle. Form into 8 patties.

Lightly coat a large pan with oil and fry for 3–4 minutes per side, or until nicely browned. The burgers will be tender straight out of the pan, but after a few minutes they will firm up.

Tips/Techniques/Substitutions

- The vital wheat gluten is optional, but it helps hold the burgers together.
- We recommend using short grain brown rice because it is stickier than long grain rice and helps to hold the burgers together. You can use any other rice, but the burgers might not hold together as well.
- Give the walnuts a quick chop by hand before adding them to the food processor. This helps to get an even crumble. Also, sort through the walnuts prior to processing as there can be pieces of the hard interior partition of the shell. They are not fun to bite down on and can damage teeth!
- The burgers can be grilled, but we recommend frying first so that an outer crust forms.
- These may be baked rather than fried, but the crust might not be as crispy.

Final Preparation & Serving Suggestions

- Serve on a bun with ketchup, mustard, pickles, lettuce and tomato, just like the classic American burger.
- We love these served up with mayonnaise, dark barbecue sauce, and pickles - a flavor combination that is addictive!

Curried Lentil Burgers

There is a restaurant in Oklahoma City that serves a really good veggie burger flavored with curry. Unfortunately, they use eggs in the mixture. This recipe features all of the warm and spicy flavors of the restaurant version but with only plant-based ingredients! It's sure to become a family favorite. **Makes 8-9 patties**

Ingredients

¼ cup pearl barley
¼ cup plus 2 tablespoons short grain brown rice
1 cup brown lentils, picked over and rinsed
3 ¼ cups water
1 tablespoon vegan butter, such as *Earth Balance*
½ medium yellow onion, chopped
1 garlic clove, minced
2–3 teaspoons fresh ginger, grated or minced
1 ½ teaspoons curry powder
3 tablespoons vital wheat gluten
3 tablespoons fresh cilantro, chopped
½ teaspoon salt
¼ –½ cup bread crumbs

Directions

Combine barley and rice in a pot with water. Bring to a boil, lower heat to a simmer, cover and cook 10 minutes. Stir in the lentils. Cover again and cook until tender, 25–35 minutes more. Remove from the heat and set aside to cool slightly.

Sauté onion in vegan butter. Add the garlic and ginger and cook about 30 seconds. Remove from heat and transfer to the bowl of a food processor. Add the cooled lentil mixture, curry powder, vital wheat gluten, cilantro and salt. Pulse until mostly smooth, leaving some texture. Taste and adjust seasoning.

Scrape mixture into a large mixing bowl and add enough breadcrumbs to achieve a slightly tacky texture. Mix thoroughly.

Cover bowl and refrigerate for at least one hour. Form into 8–9 patties. Spray a skillet lightly with vegetable oil and brown patties over medium heat, 2–3 minutes per side.

Tips/Techniques/Substitutions

- We recommend using short grain brown rice because it is stickier than long grain rice and helps to hold the burgers together. You can use any other type of rice, but the burgers might not hold together as well.
- You can grill the burgers, but we recommend frying first so that an outer crust forms.
- These can be baked rather than fried, but the crust might not be as crispy.

Final Preparation & Serving Suggestions

- Like the *Black Bean Burgers* (page 72), these are so flavorful on their own that you don't need any condiments. A smear of vegan "mayo" with some lettuce and tomato in a wrap or on a toasted bun is delicious. Or, enjoy with avocado, slices of vegan cheese, or a mound of cole slaw.
- Top with fresh mango slices, mango salsa or grilled pineapple slices.
- Serve crumbled or chopped on top of a salad.

Curried
Lentil
Burgers

Seitan
Tofu
Bologna

Seitan Tofu Bologna

There's something comforting about a simple bologna sandwich. Most likely it harkens back to having them for lunch when we were kids. Just because we grow up and go vegan doesn't mean we have to do without. Try this...you'll see. **Makes 6-8 servings**

Ingredients

1 ½ cups vital wheat gluten
¼ cup nutritional yeast
¼ cup almond meal
1 14-ounce package extra-firm tofu, pressed and drained
2 teaspoons sweet paprika
2 teaspoons onion powder
2 teaspoons garlic powder
1 teaspoon salt
¼ teaspoon ground cumin
1 tablespoon vegetable oil
1 tablespoon vegan Worcestershire sauce
1 tablespoon ketchup
1 tablespoon tomato paste
¼ teaspoon liquid smoke
¼ cup water, or more as needed

Directions

Place a steamer basket in a large pot with enough water to just reach the bottom of the basket, but don't heat the water just yet.

In a medium-sized bowl, stir together the dry ingredients. In a small bowl, whisk together the wet ingredients. Pour the wet ingredients into the dry and stir, adding more water if needed, to create a moist, pliable dough. Knead 1–2 minutes. Taste and adjust seasonings.

Divide the dough in half and shape each piece into 6" logs. Wrap each log in aluminum foil and twist the ends, leaving some room for expansion as the bologna cooks. Bring the water in the pot to a boil, then turn down the heat to a simmer. Place foil-wrapped bologna in the steamer basket, cover pot and cook sausages for 40 minutes.

Heat oven to 350-degrees F. Carefully transfer the logs (do not unwrap) to a baking sheet and bake for 10 minutes. Let the bologna cool slightly before storing in the refrigerator until ready to use.

Tips/Techniques/Substitutions

- Almond meal can be purchased at most grocery stores, or grind whole or slivered almonds in a food processor. Don't over process or you will make almond butter!

Final Preparation & Serving Suggestions

- Pile high on bread slices and add lettuce and vegan mayonnaise.
- Slather with barbecue sauce and heat in a pan. Then serve as is, or make a barbecue bologna sandwich.
- Slice, pan fry and serve as a side at breakfast.
- Slice into rounds and serve on an appetizer platter with vegan cheese slices and cut up vegetables.

Portobello Mushroom Burgers

A quick and easy lunch or dinner, these burgers are so flavorful you will never miss the meat. **Serves 4**

Ingredients

4 large portobello mushrooms, cleaned and stems removed
½ cup olive oil
4 tablespoons red wine vinegar
2 cloves garlic, minced
3 teaspoons dried thyme

Directions

Whisk the olive oil, vinegar, garlic and thyme together in a small bowl. Place the mushroom caps in a large resealable gallon-sized freezer bag and pour in the marinade. Marinate for 45 minutes, turning every 15 minutes or so.

Remove mushrooms from the marinade and grill them on a gas or charcoal grill over medium heat for about 6 minutes per side. You can also prepare on a stove top pan over medium heat.

Reserve the marinade for serving.

Tips/Techniques/Substitutions

*   These burgers can be really moist, especially when cooked on the stove top. This can result in a soggy bun. To help avoid this, toast a sturdy bun and assemble sandwich so that there is lettuce on both sides of the mushroom.
*   Removing the gills from the mushroom prior to marinating will also help reduce moisture.

Final Preparation & Serving Suggestions

*   Place grilled mushroom cap on a toasted bun with vegan mayo, shredded vegan mozzarella cheese and baby mixed greens. Drizzle with some of the reserved marinade.
*   Slice and serve over salad, or arrange slices on an appetizer tray.
*   Enjoy this as a mushroom "steak" alongside oven-baked potatoes and steamed vegetables and steak sauce.

Chickpea Tuna Fish

This is one of the easiest and fastest recipes in this book to prepare. Chickpeas are a great low-fat source of protein and since the mayonnaise is used sparingly, this recipe is almost guilt-free! **Serves 2**

Ingredients

1 15-ounce can of chickpeas, rinsed and drained
2 tablespoons vegan mayonnaise (such as *Just Mayo* or *Vegenaise*)
1 teaspoon wet yellow mustard
1 teaspoon dill pickle juice
½ cup celery, finely chopped
2 tablespoons shredded, minced carrot
1–2 tablespoons dill pickle, finely chopped

Directions

In the bowl of a food processor, pulse the chickpeas until chopped. Be careful not to overprocess; leave some texture.

In a small mixing bowl, whisk together the mayonnaise, mustard and dill pickle juice. Add the processed chickpeas to the mixing bowl and stir to combine. Stir in the remaining ingredients. Taste and adjust seasoning.

Tips/Techniques/Substitutions

*   The chickpeas out of the can should be firm. If the chickpeas are very soft, the extra moisture will dilute the flavors of the other ingredients.
*   This recipe can be easily customized to your personal taste and desire to experiment! Add more pickle juice, less celery, and/or try different kinds of mustard.
*   The water (or "aquafaba") from the can of chickpeas can be reserved and used as an egg replacement in baked goods.

Final Preparation & Serving Suggestions

*   Make a classic "tuna fish" sandwich with fresh lettuce and tomato slices.
*   Top your favorite cracker for a satisfying afternoon snack!
*   Mix into cooked pasta or make a "tuna" casserole.

Tofu Tawook

... or "taouk") is traditionally a Middle Eastern dish where meat is ... and then grilled, often on a kebab. There are many variations ... the marinade but they often include garlic, tomato paste, lemon juice and spices. Here is our veg-friendly take on the dish. **Serves 4**

Ingredients

1 14-ounce package extra-firm tofu, drained and pressed
2–3 tablespoons olive oil
2 tablespoons fresh lemon juice
1 tablespoon apple cider vinegar
½ teaspoon tomato paste
2 garlic cloves, minced
¼ teaspoon sweet paprika
¼ teaspoon ground cumin
¼ teaspoon dried thyme (or dried oregano)
¼ teaspoon black pepper
¼ teaspoon salt

Directions

Slice the tofu into small cubes, about a half-inch in size. Set aside.

Combine all the remaining ingredients for the marinade. Toss the tofu cubes with the marinade. Cover and refrigerate for at least one hour, or up to overnight.

Remove from the refrigerator and sauté the tofu with the marinade in a skillet or saucepan until slightly browned, about 10 minutes.

Tips/Techniques/Substitutions

* It is not necessary to add oil to the pan when sautéing as there is plenty in the marinade.
* Keep it super simple and skip the sautéing step. The marinated tofu tastes great as is!

Final Preparation & Serving Suggestions

* Spread a tortilla with hummus, add dill pickle slices and top with tawook for a quick and easy lunch. _Pita !_
* Tofu tawook makes a great addition to a green salad.

TVP Ham Salad

If ham salad was one of your favorite childhood dishes, you're in luck! This easy plant-based dish has all of the smoky, salty flavors you remember – while being healthy and cruelty-free. This is a simple, but satisfying dish that takes almost no time at all to make. **Serves 4-6**

Ingredients

1 cup Textured Vegetable Protein (TVP)
2 tablespoons liquid smoke, plus boiling water to equal $7/8$ cup
1 teaspoon salt
$1/2$ teaspoon ground black pepper
6 tablespoons vegan mayonnaise (such as *Just Mayo* or *Vegenaise*)
1 $1/2$ tablespoons sweet pickle relish
1–2 teaspoons beet juice for color, optional

Directions

Place TVP in a medium-sized bowl. Pour the boiling water/liquid smoke mixture over the TVP and let sit for 10 minutes to reconstitute. If the mixture seems wet, use a paper towel to squeeze out the excess moisture after the 10 minutes have passed.

Mix in the mayonnaise. If you prefer a smoother ham salad, place in a food processor and pulse until the desired texture is achieved. If you have processed the mixture, place it back in the bowl before adding the sweet pickle relish and mix well. Taste for seasoning and add salt and/or pepper as needed. For a more authentic color, stir in the beet juice.

Chill salad for at least 2 hours in the refrigerator to allow the flavors to meld.

Final Preparation & Serving Suggestions

• This makes a delicious sandwich filling.
• Serve with crackers and cut up veggies for a light lunch.
• Cut off the tops of cherry tomatoes, hollow them out and fill with TVP Ham Salad for a simple appetizer.

Tofu Hot Dogs

If you loved hot dogs as a kid but stopped eating them as an adult once you learned that they contained less-than-healthy ingredients, we have good news for you! You can easily make delicious plant-based hot dogs at home. Knowing what goes into them means guilt-free enjoyment!
Makes 8 hot dogs

Ingredients

1/3 cup low-sodium vegetable broth
1 teaspoon cornstarch
5 tablespoons almond meal
9 ounces extra-firm silken tofu
1 tablespoon tomato paste
1 tablespoon onion powder
1 tablespoon smoked paprika
1 teaspoon sugar
1 teaspoon salt
1 teaspoon garlic powder
1 teaspoon dry mustard powder
½ teaspoon ground coriander
½ teaspoon liquid smoke
1 cup vital wheat gluten

Directions

Place a steamer basket in a large pot with enough water to just reach the bottom of the basket, but don't heat the water just yet.

In a small bowl or measuring cup, whisk together the cornstarch and vegetable broth. Cut eight, 4-inch x 10-inch pieces of parchment paper. Tear off eight, 4-inch x 10-inch pieces of aluminum foil. Set aside.

To the bowl of a food processor, add the almond meal, tofu, tomato paste, spices and liquid smoke and process until smooth. With the processor running, slowly pour in the water/cornstarch mixture. Process until thoroughly combined. Scrape the mixture into a medium-sized bowl. Stir in the vital wheat gluten and knead for 2–3 minutes.

Divide the dough into eight pieces and roll each into 6" hot dog shapes. Wrap hot dogs in parchment paper, leaving a little room for expansion as they cook. Twist the ends and then wrap in aluminum foil.

Bring the water in the pot to a boil, then turn down the heat to a gentle simmer. Place foil-wrapped hot dogs in the steamer basket, cover pot and cook for 50 minutes.

Let hot dogs cool slightly before carefully unwrapping and serving. Store leftovers in an air-tight container in the refrigerator.

Final Preparation & Serving Suggestions

- Serve as is, or lightly grilled, on a hot dog bun.
- Top with chili, chopped onions, and shredded vegan cheddar cheese for a chili dog.

Photos of Tofu Hot Dogs on pages 94-95.

Breakfast

Breakfast Sausage Patties
Tofu Egg Cakes
Tofu Scrambled Egg
Cashew and Tofu Quiche
Tempeh Bacon

Breakfast Sausage Patties

A good breakfast sets the tone for the rest of the day. Breakfast used to mean eggs, toast and sausage or bacon. Nowadays, vegans don't need to miss out on "traditional" morning fare. We can enjoy tofu scrambles, omelets, even biscuits with sausage gravy! There are commercial vegan breakfast sausages available, but they're expensive and contain way too many ingredients – including preservatives and other additives. These savory sausage patties come together in minutes. **Makes 8-10 patties**

Ingredients

½ cup Textured Vegetable Protein (TVP)
½ cup plus 1 tablespoon low-sodium vegetable broth, divided
½ cup cooked brown rice
1 tablespoon yellow onion, roughly chopped
3 tablespoons water
1 tablespoon flaxseed meal
1 ½ teaspoons poultry seasoning
¾ teaspoon ground black pepper
½ teaspoon garlic powder
½ teaspoon fennel seeds, crushed or lightly chopped
½ teaspoon salt
1 ½ teaspoons pure maple syrup
2 tablespoons vital wheat gluten

Directions

Preheat oven to 350-degrees F and lightly oil a baking sheet (or use parchment paper). Set aside.

Place the TVP in a medium bowl. Bring ½ cup of vegetable broth to a boil and pour over the TVP. Let sit 10 minutes to reconstitute.

Prepare an "egg" binder by whisking the flaxseed meal with the 3 tablespoons water in a small bowl. Set aside to thicken.

In a food processor, pulse rice and onion with the remaining 1 tablespoon broth until lightly chopped. Transfer mixture to the bowl with the TVP and add the poultry seasoning, black pepper, garlic powder, fennel seeds and salt. Stir to combine. Stir in the flax "egg" and the maple syrup, followed by the vital wheat gluten. Mix well with a spoon.

Form mixture into 8–10, two-inch patties and place on the prepared baking sheet. Bake for 18–20 minutes, flipping patties halfway through baking time. Alternatively, pan fry patties in about one tablespoon of oil in a large pan over medium heat for 4–5 minutes per side, or until brown and cooked through.

Tips/Techniques/Substitutions

* Use a mortar and pestle to crush the fennel seeds, or use the bottom of a heavy glass on a cutting board. You can also use a coffee grinder to quickly crush seeds.
* There are many brands of poultry seasoning on the market and they can contain different blends of spices. We recommend one that contains thyme, sage, marjoram and rosemary - or make your own blend.

Final Preparation & Serving Suggestions

* Serve patties on the side with *Tofu Scrambled Egg* (page 104), or chop and stir into your favorite scramble!
* Make into larger (~3-inch) patties, cook and serve on toasted English muffins with *Tofu Egg Cakes* (page 102) and vegan cheese for a delightful breakfast sandwich.

Breakfast
Sausage
Patties

Tofu
Egg
Cakes

Tofu Egg Cakes

Many of us grew up enjoying eggs at breakfast. Admittedly this recipe is not an exact substitute for the taste and texture of a fried or even a scrambled egg. However, as you transition to a plant-based diet you will find that there are endless choices for every meal that don't rely on animal products. These easy, non-dairy eggs are a great example of the deliciousness of cruelty-free food! **Makes 6-8 cakes**

Ingredients

1 tablespoon nutritional yeast
½ teaspoon turmeric
½ teaspoon salt (see Tips)
4 teaspoons cornstarch
1/8 teaspoon baking powder
1 14-ounce package extra-firm tofu, pressed and drained
1 tablespoon tahini
½ teaspoon Dijon mustard
Vegetable oil or olive oil, for cooking

Directions

Whisk together the dry ingredients in a small bowl and set aside.

In the bowl of a food processor, process the tofu, tahini and mustard until smooth. Add the dry ingredients and process until thoroughly combined. The mixture will be thick.

Heat a large non-stick pan or cast iron skillet over medium-heat. Coat the pan lightly with oil and drop 1/3 to ½ cup of the mixture into the pan. Gently smooth out so that it looks like a pancake. Continue with the remaining batter. Don't crowd the pan. You may need to cook these in batches.

Cook egg cakes 4–5 minutes per side, or until they are nicely browned and firm. Serve immediately.

Tips/Techniques/Substitutions

- These eggs don't cook quickly like chicken eggs. After 8–10 minutes, the eggs will be cooked inside, and will have a smooth, silky texture.
- Take this recipe up a notch by using "black salt" (a.k.a. *kala namak*) instead of regular salt. See more on this ingredient in the **Groceries** chapter (page 14).

Final Preparation & Serving Suggestions

- Make an "egg" sandwich with toast, English muffin, or bagel.
- Wrap in a tortilla with *Tempeh Bacon* (page 110), sliced avocado, salsa, and other fixings.
- Chop and mix into potato salad.
- Sauté some green onions, mushrooms, jalapeños, spinach, red pepper, or other vegetables, then drop tofu egg batter over the veggies and cook as described above.

Tofu Scrambled Egg

This recipe more than any other showcases the magic of tofu, turmeric, and a little patience. In just a few minutes, scrambled "eggs" will appear before your eyes! **Serves 2**

Ingredients

1 14-ounce package extra-firm tofu, drained and pressed well
2 teaspoons nutritional yeast
$\frac{1}{2}$ teaspoon turmeric
$\frac{1}{4}$ teaspoon onion powder
$\frac{1}{4}$ teaspoon salt (see Tips)
$\frac{1}{4}$ teaspoon sweet paprika
1 $\frac{1}{2}$ tablespoons non-dairy butter
2 tablespoons unsweetened non-dairy milk

Directions

Press the tofu for an hour or more (see **Techniques** section starting on page 20 for a how-to). For this recipe, it is important that the tofu be is as dense as possible so that it holds together during cooking. After pressing, slice into 1/8-inch wide strips. The slices don't have to be perfect because they will break up during cooking.

Combine the seasonings in a small bowl. In a skillet, melt the butter over medium heat. Stir in the seasonings and the milk. Stir for about 1 minute to make a sauce.

Add the tofu. Turn the heat up to medium-high. With a metal spatula, alternate gently separating the tofu slices, distributing the sauce, and then letting the slices sit to cook. Continue cooking for 8–10 minutes, depending on how moist or dry you want the scramble.

Tips/Techniques/Substitutions

- Don't start with a skillet that is too hot. This will cause the butter and seasonings to clump and cook before the tofu is added.
- The dry ingredients for this recipe can be made ahead of time in a large batch. For each block of tofu you cook, measure out 3 ¼ teaspoons of the blend and whisk into the milk and vegan butter.
- Just like *Tofu Egg Cakes* recipe (page 102), try substituting "black salt" for regular salt for an egg-y aroma and taste.

Final Preparation & Serving Suggestions

- Make a breakfast burrito with salsa and non-dairy cheese.
- Sauté some vegetables and stir into the scramble near the end of the cooking time.

Tofu
Scrambled
Egg

Cashew
and Tofu
Quiche

Cashew and Tofu Quiche

This recipe has undergone quite a transformation in the last several years. The original version consisted mainly of tofu instead of eggs, but the flavor and texture needed work. We added cashews, tweaked the seasonings, and adjusted the baking technique. *Voila!* Your new favorite quiche recipe for breakfast, brunch, or anytime! **Serves 6-8**

Ingredients

1 9-inch pie shell, unbaked
1 tablespoon olive oil
1 yellow onion, chopped
1 garlic clove, finely chopped
2 cups broccoli florets, chopped
1/4 cup raw cashews, soaked and drained
1/4 –1/2 cup unsweetened non-dairy milk
10 ounces extra-firm tofu, pressed, drained and cut into chunks
1/4 cup nutritional yeast
1 teaspoon salt
1 teaspoon dried basil
1/2 teaspoon turmeric
1/8 teaspoon baking powder
Ground black pepper, to taste
1/2 cup non-dairy cheddar cheese shreds, optional

Directions

Preheat oven to 400-degrees F.

Heat olive oil in a skillet over medium heat and sauté onions and garlic until translucent, about 2 minutes. Add broccoli and cook until it is crisp tender, 8–10 minutes.

Process cashews with the milk in a food processor or blender until very smooth, scraping the sides as necessary. Add the tofu, nutritional yeast, salt, basil, turmeric and baking powder and blend until creamy.

In a bowl combine the broccoli mixture with the tofu mixture and season with black pepper to taste. Stir in the cheese, if using. Pour mixture into the crust and spread evenly. If desired, top with tomato slices.

Bake for 45–50 minutes, or until a knife inserted just off center comes out clean.

Tips/Techniques/Substitutions
- Check crust after 35 minutes. Cover with aluminum foil to prevent it from getting too brown.
- Just like the *Tofu Egg Cakes* recipe (page 102), substitute "black salt" (*kala namak*) for the regular salt.

Final Preparation & Serving Suggestions
- Instead of broccoli, try these other tasty combinations:
  - green bell pepper, mushroom, and diced green chiles
  - asparagus and mushroom
  - spinach and red bell pepper
- For a smoky flavor, substitute non-dairy gouda for the cheddar.

Additional photo of Cashew and Tofu Quiche on page 132.

Tempeh Bacon

Prepared plant-based bacons available at grocery stores offer convenience, but they are often too salty, not to mention expensive. This recipe has all of the smoky, bacony flavor of the "real" thing with the added bonus of being made with cruelty-free, nutritious tempeh. **Makes 16-18 strips**

Ingredients

2 tablespoons low-sodium soy sauce
2 teaspoons apple cider vinegar
2 teaspoons barbecue sauce or ketchup
$\frac{1}{4}$–$\frac{1}{2}$ teaspoon liquid smoke
$\frac{1}{4}$ teaspoon garlic powder
1 8-ounce package tempeh
Vegetable oil, for frying

Directions

Stir together the soy sauce, vinegar, barbecue sauce, liquid smoke and garlic powder in an 8-inch x 11-inch baking dish. Slice the tempeh into $\frac{1}{4}$-inch wide strips. Dip each slice in the marinade and arrange in a single layer in the baking dish. You should have just enough marinade with a little left over.

Cover and put the baking dish in the refrigerator and marinate for at least an hour. When ready to cook, fry in vegetable oil over medium-high heat, flipping strips over after the first side is browned, about 2–3 minutes per side. Watch closely so they don't burn. Serve immediately or store in an air-tight container in the refrigerator until ready to use.

Tips/Techniques/Substitutions

*   Marinate tempeh overnight in the refrigerator so it is ready to cook in the morning.
*   Strips about 4" long are easy to manage without breaking.
*   There are dozens of other plant-based recipes out there for bacon using ingredients like coconut, rice paper, tofu, and eggplant. Tempeh is an excellent choice for the right balance of savory/sweet/salty without being too fragile.

Final Preparation & Serving Suggestions

*   Serve at breakfast with *Tofu Egg Cakes* (page 102).
*   Wrap in a tortilla with *Tofu Scrambled Egg* (page 104), avocado, salsa, and other fixings.
*   These strips are perfect for BLAT (bacon, lettuce, avocado and tomato) sandwiches.
*   Coarsely chop and sprinkle on top of green salads or into potato salads.

Cheeses

Tofu Feta Cheese
Nutty Parmesan Topping
Creamy Tofu Ricotta
Cashew Cheese Sauce

Tofu Feta Cheese

Other vegan feta cheese recipes call for baking the tofu. Some add the extra step of boiling the marinade. For a quick, fuss-free recipe, this one is hard to beat for flavor and ease of preparation. **Makes 2 cups**

Ingredients

2 teaspoons olive oil
3 tablespoons fresh lemon juice
1 ½ tablespoons white wine vinegar
½ teaspoon salt
½ teaspoon dried oregano
¼ teaspoon garlic powder
1 14-ounce package extra-firm tofu, pressed well and drained

Directions

Whisk together the olive oil, lemon juice, vinegar, salt and spices. With your hands, crumble tofu (or break into chunks) into the bowl and toss with the marinade. Let mixture sit at room temperature for about one hour. Taste and adjust seasonings.

Store in an air-tight container in the refrigerator.

Tips/Techniques/Substitutions

* Be sure to press out most of the liquid from the tofu before crumbling it into the marinade so that the flavors are not diluted.
* The longer the tofu marinates, the more flavors it absorbs.

Final Preparation & Serving Suggestions

* Toss into green salads.
* Use it to garnish soups.
* Stir into roasted vegetables.
* Sprinkle onto open-faced sandwiches.
* Serve as an appetizer with flatbread and/or crackers.

Nutty Parmesan Topping

This recipe is largely based on the cheesy flavor of nutritional yeast. If you have not used nutritional yeast before, it can be an "acquired taste". Chances are, though, it won't be long before you are sprinkling this topping on everything and making it in large batches to have some on hand at all times! **Makes about 1 1/2 cups**

Ingredients

¼ cup + 2 tablespoons raw pepitas (pumpkin seeds)
¼ cup + 2 tablespoons raw walnuts, roughly chopped
½ cup nutritional yeast
½ teaspoon garlic powder
½ teaspoon onion powder or flakes
¼ teaspoon salt

Directions

Pulse the pepitas in the bowl of a food processor until coarsely chopped. Add the walnuts and process to a crumbly texture. Do not over process. Pour mixture into a small mixing bowl and stir in remaining ingredients.

Store in an air-tight container in the refrigerator.

Tips/Techniques/Substitutions

* This keeps well in the refrigerator so you can make it in large batches.
* The seeds/nuts can be swapped for different varieties, such as almonds, sunflower seeds, pecans or cashews.
* This recipe boasts rich Parmesan flavor, but will *not* melt or provide moistness when baked or heated.

Final Preparation & Serving Suggestions

* Serve as a topping for Italian dishes such as spaghetti with marinara sauce.
* Sprinkle on top of pizza.
* Toss into salads.
* Sprinkle over popcorn.

Creamy Tofu Ricotta

It can be a struggle to go without dairy cheese in the first few months after going vegan. Hummus and other plant-based dips can be good substitutes...sometimes. But for those other times – when you want something creamy, tangy and cheesy – this tofu ricotta completely satisfies.
Makes about 2 cups

Ingredients

½ cup raw cashews
¼ cup fresh lemon juice
¾ teaspoon salt
2 tablespoons olive oil
1 14-ounce package extra-firm tofu, pressed, drained and crumbled

Directions

In the bowl of a food processor, pulse the cashews with the lemon juice, olive oil and salt. The cashews should be of a crumbled consistency to add texture to the ricotta.

Add in the tofu and pulse until well blended.

Tips/Techniques/Substitutions

* Give the ricotta Italian flavor by mixing in some garlic powder and/or dried basil.
* For more of a cream cheese flavor, omit the olive oil and add ¾ teaspoon of sugar.

Final Preparation & Serving Suggestions

* Use this anywhere you would use dairy ricotta, such as in lasagna, stuffed shells, manicotti, or sprinkled on top of pasta.
* Spread it on a baguette with roasted vegetables to make a delicious sandwich.

Cashew Cheese Sauce

There are many recipes for vegan cheese sauces, but few are as quick, easy, and versatile as this one. In no time this will be your "go-to" recipe for adding rich cheesy flavor to snacks and other dishes. **Makes about 2 cups**

Ingredients

¼ cup raw cashews, soaked in water
1 ½ cups water
½ roasted red bell pepper (see Tips)
2 tablespoons cornstarch
2 tablespoons nutritional yeast
1 tablespoon fresh lemon juice
½ teaspoon salt

Directions

Drain the cashews and process them in a high-speed blender with ½ cup of the water until very smooth. Add the rest of the ingredients, including the remaining 1 cup water, and blend again to puree the pepper and thoroughly mix everything together.

Transfer mixture to a saucepan. Cook over medium heat until very thick, 6–7 minutes, stirring constantly.

Serve immediately or store in an air-tight container in the refrigerator until ready to use.

Tips/Techniques/Substitutions
* Use with anything Tex-Mex such as nachos, tacos, enchiladas and burritos.
* Serve as a dip with crackers or vegetables.
* Stir into cooked pasta for a quick mac 'n cheese.
* Use in casseroles that call for melted cheese.

Final Preparation & Serving Suggestions
* If you don't have a high-speed blender (such as a *Vitamix* or a *Blendtec*), you can use a regular blender. Soak the cashews in water for 2 or more days in the refrigerator. Cover cashews with plenty of water because they will expand in size. The ¼ cup measure is the volume before soaking.
* Use bottled roasted red bell peppers or easily roast your own: Slice pepper in half, remove the seeds and membranes and place pieces on a baking sheet under a broiler for 2-3 minutes. Watch closely! Place pieces in a small bowl, cover and let sit for about 10 minutes so that the skin loosens, making removal easier. Discard skins.
* If a "skin" develops on the bottom of the pan while cooking the mixture on the stovetop, turn the heat down a notch.
* For nacho cheese sauce, stir in some diced green chiles or salsa. These will thin the sauce a bit, but makes for a fantastic combination of flavors.
* Tapioca starch can be substituted for cornstarch. Tapioca starch will result in a glossier, slightly smoother sauce. The ratio of substitution is 2 parts tapioca for 1 part cornstarch. A recommended blend is 1½ tablespoons cornstarch + 1 tablespoon tapioca starch.
* The sauce will thicken after refrigeration. A quick reheat in the microwave will restore the smooth, creamy consistency.

Photos of Cashew Cheese Sauce on pages 122-123.

When You Don't Want to COOK

Let's face it. There are some days when you have neither the time nor inclination to cook. Thankfully, there are *loads* of meat and cheese alternatives available at grocery stores these days, and more being introduced all the time. Yes, these convenience items are in the "processed" category and yes, they can be more expensive than making them at home, but for those days when you need some help at mealtimes, these timesavers are a real treat! Below are some brands we use and like. All of these freeze well, so when you see a sale, stock up!

MEATS

Tofurky
Italian Sausage
Andouille Sausage
Chick'n Apple Sausage
Spinach Pesto Sausage
Oven Roasted Deli Slices
Bologna Deli Slices

Gardein
Seven Grain Crispy Tenders
Chick'n Scallopini
Beefless Ground
Homestyle Beefless Tips
Holiday Roast
Crabless Cakes

Beyond Meat
Beyond Chicken Strips
Beyond Beef Crumbles

Field Roast
Smoked Apple Sage Sausage
Mexican Chipotle Sausage
Italian Sausage

Sweet Earth
Traditional & Chipotle Ground
Traditional & Chipotle Strips
Veggie Burgers
Tuscan Veggie Sausage & Benevolent Bacon
Curry Satay

Upton's Naturals
Original Seitan
Bacon Seitan
Chorizo Seitan

Lightlife
Gimme Lean Sausage

Yves
Meatless Ground Crumbles

Engine 2 Diet
Italian Fennel Burgers
Pinto Habanero Burgers
Tuscan Kale White Bean Burgers

CHEESES

Daiya
Shredded mozzarella, cheddar, and pepper jack

Follow Your Heart
A variety of shredded, sliced, and block cheeses such as mozzarella, cheddar, smoked gouda, pepper jack, American, and provolone

Chao (by Field Roast)
Creamy Original Slices, Tomato Cayenne Slices

PREPARED MEALS

There are many excellent plant-based frozen prepared meals and canned soups available at most grocery stores. Before you start loading up the grocery cart though, a word of caution: *Check the ingredients to make sure they are 100% vegan.*

Amy's
Canned soups, chili, frozen entrées, and frozen burritos

Kashi
Frozen vegetable and grain bowls

Daiya
Frozen pizza

Sweet Earth
Frozen entrées and frozen burritos

Beyond Meat
Frozen entrées

RESTAURANTS

When even heating up a frozen entrée feels like too much work and you really just want *someone else* to prepare your meal, we have a few tips for restaurant dining.

Before heading out, check *HappyCow* (happycow.net). Founded in 1999 by vegans and vegetarians who wanted to assist others in finding plant-based options for dining out, *HappyCow* is an excellent resource of vegan- and vegetarian-friendly restaurants all over the world. Just type in the city name for a list of user-reviewed restaurants and health food stores in the area. Become a member and add your own finds and reviews!

Is there a restaurant you've wanted to try but don't think they have vegan options? Don't give up! Call ahead, check the menu, or ask the waiter for suggestions. Some restaurants have a separate plant-based menu (often paired with a gluten-free menu) or have a chef who is open to preparing a special meal. The more that we ask, the more restaurants will be encouraged to add vegan dishes to their menus.

Even fast food restaurants are adding vegan options as the demand for healthier foods increases. Currently, the chains listed below offer several choices. (For most dishes you will have to request "no cheese"):

- *Taco Bell* (bean burritos)
- *Subway* (veggie sub, minestrone soup)
- *Chipotle* (sofritos bowl, bean burrito)
- *Panera* (Mediterranean veggie sandwich, black bean soup, vegetable soup)
- *Quizno's* (veggie guacamole sub)
- *Noodles & Company* (Japanese Pan Noodles)
- *Au Bon Pain* (soups and vegetarian chili)
- *Genghis Grill* (build your own stir fry with veggies and tofu)

Acknowledgements

For me, this cookbook has in a way been many years in the making. It is a testament to all those who have influenced, guided and inspired me. I have always had an enormous compassion for animals and the environment, but it wasn't until watching the *Forks Over Knives* documentary that I had the confidence to go vegan. From there, all the talented vegan friends, chefs, and activists have been a huge support along the way. I think I can speak for all three of us when I say these individuals deserve mention:

Isa Chandra Moskowitz: vegan chef and activist extraordinaire; author, columnist, cooking show host, blogger at *Post Punk Kitchen*, and owner of the plant-based restaurant located in Omaha, NE, *Modern Love*.

Aubry and Kale Walch: *The Herbivorous Butchers*

Skye Michael Conroy, Celine Steen, Joni Marie Newman, Roberto Martin, and Rip Esselstyn: chefs/bloggers/cookbook authors/activists/podcasters

The Vegetarian Society of Tulsa: I've learned so much from this group and met so many wonderful people!

In particular, starting last year in September, getting this cookbook developed and published has been very much a group effort. Many thanks to all our fearless recipe testers! Special thanks to Cindy Bergin, Phil Black and Alison Frisby for all your hard work.

And last but not least, to my loving husband, who had the courage to join me in this vegan journey and has happily accepted being a taste tester/guinea pig over all these years!

- Elaine

I am very thankful for Elaine and Annie and their enormous amount of work that went in to this cookbook. And to all of the wonderful recipe testers!

I hope everyone enjoys cooking and eating these dishes as much a we do!

- Libby

My appreciation and admiration to the innovators, entrepreneurs, bloggers, chefs and recipe developers who have helped bring veganism into the mainstream and into homes, supermarkets and restaurants all over the world - including here in cattle-rich Flyover Country. Life for vegans just keeps getting better and more delicious every day.

Thanks to Elaine and Libby for showing even this seasoned vegan new techniques and skills for making plant-based meats at home and for pushing me to write and photograph my best for this labor of love. They were the creative drive behind the recipes in this book.

Gratitude to our stalwart recipe testers who honestly shared their thoughts and suggestions that made each and every one of these recipes just that much better.

Big love to my unbelievably supportive husband, Kel. His generous spirit allows me to pursue all kinds of crazy dreams. Finally, endless belly rubs to our two furry, four-legged children, Ike and Willa, without whom our lives would be very empty indeed.

- Annie

Elaine Spencer

Elaine is an animal advocate, a running enthusiast, and loves all things outdoors. To fuel her activities, and to the delight of her family and friends, she enjoys spending time in the kitchen.

Over the years she had amassed a collection of "ultimate" recipes - ones that she has tweaked and adjusted to be The Best. That is until 2010 when she watched the *Forks Over Knives* documentary, decided to go vegan, and determined that most of the recipes needed makeovers to be plant-based.

The cooking, experimenting and perfecting continues, along with sharing the knowledge and experiences that go along with it.

Libby Doughty

Libby developed a love of cooking at an early age that has stayed with her all of her life. Her kitchen is her comfort zone, and she is in her element when preparing or developing new dishes. She loves to veganize recipes from her pre-plant-based life. Libby finds it exciting to have so many products and techniques available to the vegan cook that make the transition to cruelty-free so much easier.

Libby was inspired by her daughters, Lora and Beth, to adopt a vegetarian lifestyle over 17 years ago. That set her on the path to eventually becoming vegan, and her love of animals and nature enforces this decision. She admits that it has not always been easy, but the rewards are bountiful.

Annie Oliverio

Self-confessed dairy cheese addicts, Annie and her husband, Kel, dedicated themselves to veganism after reading *The China Study* and *Fast Food Nation* and watching *Forks Over Knives*. They firmly believe that a plant-based diet provides optimum health while infinitely expanding the depth, variety and deliciousness of one's diet. Along with this dietary change came a new respect and dedication to the rights of those without a voice or vote: animals.

Annie has authored several books and e-books, including *Crave Eat Heal: Plant-based, Whole Food Recipes to Satisfy Every Appetite, A Terminal Illness Primer for Caregivers: Lessons From My Brother's End-of-Life Journey, TEAse Me: 15 Plant-based Recipes Inspired By The World's Favorite Beverage,* and *Good Pasture: Short & Shorter Stories From Rural Oklahoma.* A second book of short stories is in the works.

For more about Annie, her books, food photography, and seven year's worth of plant-based recipes, please visit her award-winning blog, *An Unrefined Vegan.com.*

CPSIA information can be obtained
at www.ICGtesting.com
Printed in the USA
FSOW03n0226141017
39716FS